DETROIT PUBLIC LIBRARY

W9-BXS-524

CHRISTMAS

DETROIT PUBLIC LIBRARY

KNAPP BRANCH LIBRARY

13330 CONANT, DETROIT, MI 48212

852-4283

DATE DUE

DEC 2 6 2000

BC-3

JUL 99

Kn

CHRISTMAS ORNAMENTS KIDS CAN MAKE

By Kathy Ross

Illustrated by Sharon Lane Holm

The Millbrook Press   Brookfield, Connecticut

For my niece Kacey,
who really loves Christmas. —K.R.

In memory of my father,
who always loved Christmas best! —S.L.H.

Library of Congress Cataloging-in-Publication Data
Ross, Kathy (Katharine Reynolds), 1948–
Christmas ornaments kids can make / Kathy Ross; illustrated by
Sharon Lane Holm.
p. cm.
Summary: Provides step-by-step instructions for making thirty
different Christmas tree ornaments.
ISBN 0-7613-0366-9 (lib. bdg.) 0-7613-0337-5 (pbk.)
1. Christmas decorations—Juvenile literature. 2. Christmas
trees—Juvenile literature. [1. Christmas decorations. 2.
Handicraft.] I. Holm, Sharon Lane, ill. II. Title.
TT900.C4R675 1998
745.594'12—dc21
97-41170 CIP AC

Copyright © 1998 Kathy Ross
Illustrations copyright © 1998 Sharon Lane Holm
All rights reserved
Printed in the United States

Published by The Millbrook Press, Inc.
2 Old New Milford Road
Brookfield, CT 06804
5 4 3 2 1

Contents

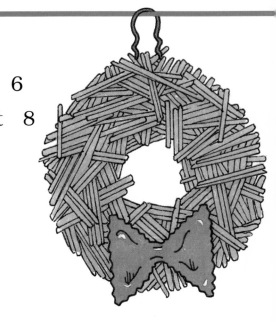

CHRISTMAS ORNAMENTS
KIDS CAN MAKE

Christmas Story Frame Ornaments

Make a series of frame ornaments to tell the Christmas story.

What you need:

old Christmas cards

foil cupcake cups

glitter

gold thread

white glue

masking tape

scissors

cereal box cardboard

construction paper

pencil

newspaper to work on

What you do:

1 Cut the bottom out of one cupcake cup. Trace the circle shape on the cereal box and cut it out to use as a pattern.

2 Find pictures on old Christmas cards to tell the Christmas story. Choose scenes that will fit in the circle pattern.

3 Use the pattern to trace around each scene. Cut out the scenes.

4 Put a strip of masking tape inside the bottom of each foil cup you will be using. This will create a better gluing surface.

5 Glue a scene in each cup. Rub glue around the edge of each scene, and sprinkle it with glitter.

6 Use the cardboard pattern to cut a construction paper circle for the back of each ornament.

7 For each ornament, cut a 5-inch (13-cm) piece of gold thread. Glue both ends of the thread to the back of the ornament so that the loop forms a hanger at the top of the scene. Glue a construction paper circle over the back of the ornament.

What a pretty way to tell the story of baby Jesus.

Santa-Down-the-Chimney Ornament

Send Santa down the chimney and back up again with this ornament.

What you need:

small sliding matchbox

red felt

fiberfill

2-inch (5-cm) tall Santa picture or sticker

scissors

masking tape

blue glue gel

green yarn

hole punch

black permanent marker

What you do:

1 Cut a piece of felt large enough to wrap and cover the outer part of the matchbox. Glue the felt in place. Use a black marker to draw bricks on the felt to make it look like a chimney.

2 Glue fiberfill around one open edge to look like snow around the top of the chimney.

3 Punch a hole in the top and bottom end of the inner box.

4 Cut a 12-inch (30-cm) piece of yarn. Fold the yarn in half and knot it together toward the two ends. Thread the yarn up through the two holes in the inner box so that the knotted end hangs out one end and the loop is at the other as a hanger for the ornament. Glue the yarn inside the box, then cover it with masking tape.

5 Glue the Santa picture inside the bottom of the box, with his head toward the loop. If you don't have a picture or sticker, you can draw your own. Put the inner box back inside the outer box.

Just pull on the bottom or top of the yarn to make Santa go up or down the chimney.

Twinkle Star

This happy little star will make your tree sparkle.

What you need:

five wooden
ice cream spoons

two large
wiggle eyes

scissors

thin ribbon

Styrofoam tray
to work on

red felt scrap

margarine tub for
mixing

gold glitter

white glue

yellow paint and
a paintbrush

What you do:

 1 Arrange the five wooden spoons in the shape of a star following the same lines you would follow if you were drawing a star without lifting your pencil.

 2 Cut a 6-inch (15-cm) piece of ribbon for a hanger.

 3 Glue the sticks together at all contact points. While the glue is still wet, slip the two ends of the hanger between the two sticks at what will be the top of the star.

 4 Mix one part glue to four parts yellow paint in the margarine tub. Paint one side of the star, then immediately sprinkle it with glitter. When the paint has dried, turn the star over and do the same thing on the other side.

 5 Choose the side of the star that you like best for the front of the ornament. Glue the two wiggle eyes on the front of the star.

6 Cut a small piece of red felt to glue over the opening at the center of the star. Glue this to the back side of the star to look like a mouth from the front.

Twinkle, Twinkle . . .

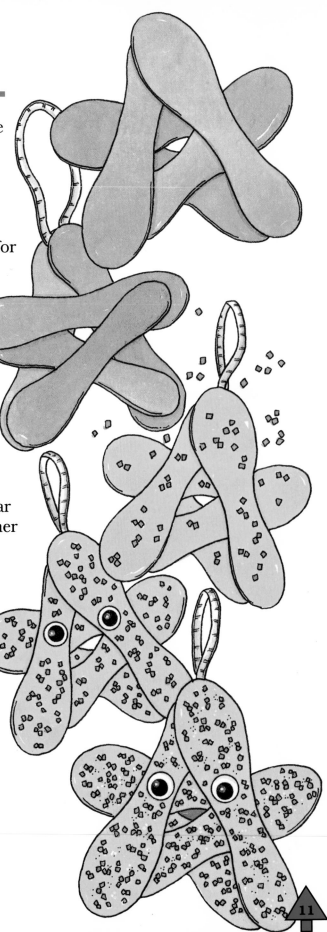

Plate Ornament

Holiday plates can be turned into adorable three-dimensional ornaments.

What you need:

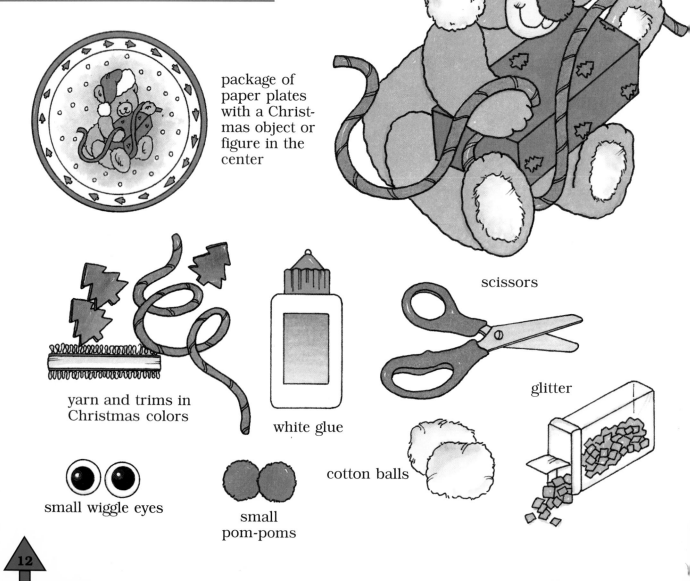

package of paper plates with a Christmas object or figure in the center

yarn and trims in Christmas colors

white glue

scissors

glitter

cotton balls

small wiggle eyes

small pom-poms

What you do:

1 Cut the figure out of the center of two identical paper plates.

2 Cut a 4-inch (10-cm) piece of yarn.

3 Cut three ½-inch (1½-cm) squares from the plate scraps and glue them together in a stack.

4 Glue the stack to the center front of one figure and the back of the other to join them together. The double figure will give the ornament a three-dimensional look. At the same time, glue the two ends of the yarn between the top of the two figures to form a hanger.

5 Decorate the front figure by highlighting it with trims, glitter, cotton, pom-poms, and wiggle eyes. What you use will depend on the picture on the plates you use. If you cut out a Christmas tree, you might want to use sequins, and if you cut out a Santa head, you could cover the beard with cotton.

Decorating plate ornaments gives you lots of room to add your own creative finishing touches!

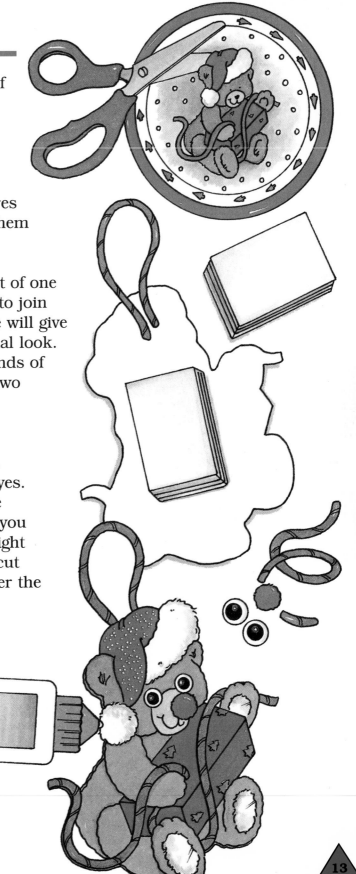

Crisscross Ornament

Crisscross ornaments are dramatic decorations for your tree.

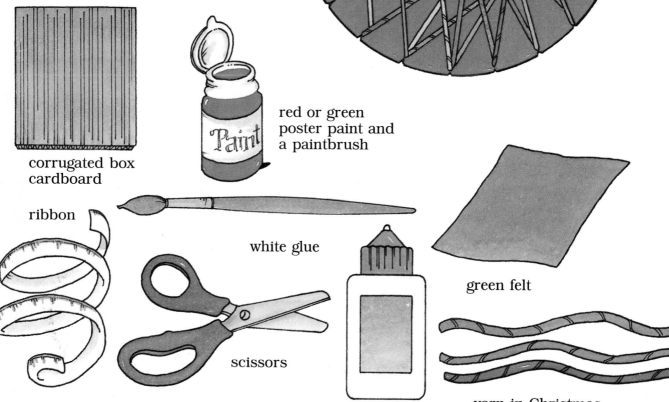

What you need:

corrugated box cardboard

red or green poster paint and a paintbrush

ribbon

white glue

green felt

scissors

yarn in Christmas colors of your choice

What you do:

 1 Cut a 4-inch (10-cm) circle from the cardboard. Cut ½-inch (1½-cm) slits all the way around the edge of the circle and about ¼ to ½ inch (½ to 1¼ cm) apart.

 2 Paint the front of the circle and let it dry.

3 Cut a piece of yarn at least 2 feet (60 cm) long. Slide one end into one of the slits. Take the yarn across the circle and slide it into another slit. Crisscross the yarn back and forth over the circle in all different angles to cover the circle with lines of yarn. When the yarn you have cut runs out, start a new piece in a different color. Keep crisscrossing the circle with different colors of yarn until you like the way it looks.

 4 Cut a 4-inch (10-cm) piece of ribbon. Glue the two ends of the ribbon to the back of the circle to form a hanger.

 5 Cut a circle of green felt 4 inches (10 cm) wide. Glue the circle to the back of the ornament to finish it.

Try lots of different color combinations of paint and yarn. You might want to add some gold trim or thin ribbon to your ornament.

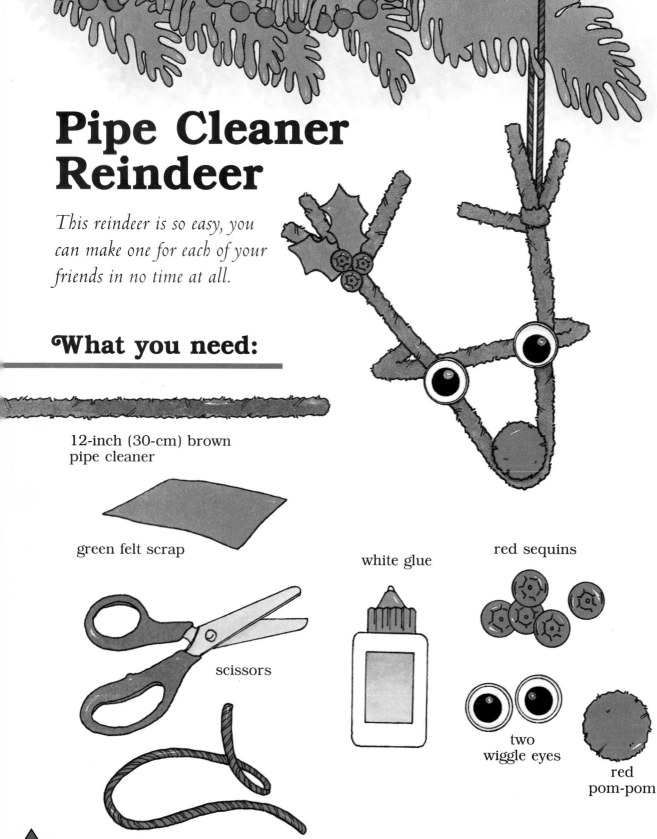

Pipe Cleaner Reindeer

This reindeer is so easy, you can make one for each of your friends in no time at all.

What you need:

12-inch (30-cm) brown pipe cleaner

green felt scrap

scissors

red embroidery floss

white glue

red sequins

two wiggle eyes

red pom-pom

What you do:

 Cut a 6-inch (15-cm) piece of brown pipe cleaner. Fold the pipe cleaner in half to form a V shape.

 Cut a second piece of pipe cleaner about 2½ inches (6 cm) long. Set the piece across the V shape about one third of the way up. Wrap the pipe cleaner once around both branches of the V. Fold the leftover ends of the second pipe cleaner back to form ears for the reindeer.

3 Cut the remaining piece of pipe cleaner in half. Wrap a piece around the top portion of each side of the V to make antler prongs for the reindeer.

4 Glue a wiggle eye on each side of the V below the ears. Glue the pom-pom nose on the point of the V.

5 Cut two holly leaves from the green felt. Glue the leaves on one antler. Glue some red sequin berries between the two leaves. Cut an 8-inch (20-cm) piece of embroidery floss. Tie it around the antler without the holly on it. Make a knot in the end of the floss to form a hanger loop.

Pipe cleaner reindeer also make very nice package decorations.

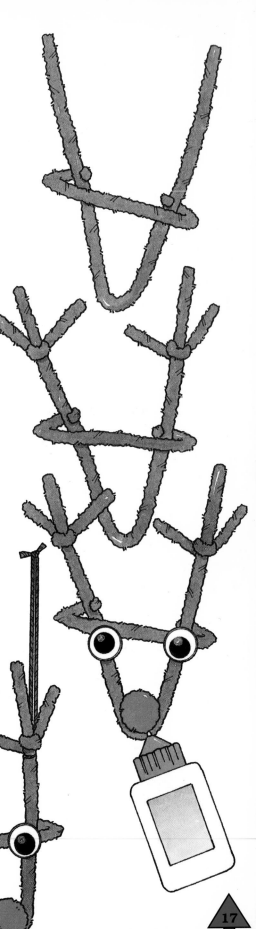

Napkin-Covered Balls

Use this idea to make beautiful Christmas tree balls.

What you need:

Christmas napkin with colorful figure or pattern

white glue

clear glitter

scissors

2½-inch (1½-cm) Styrofoam ball

paintbrush

newspaper to work on

pipe cleaner

margarine tub for mixing

Styrofoam egg carton for drying

What you do:

1 Choose the part of the napkin that you wish to be on the front of your ornament. Center your main design on the ball and wrap the napkin around the ball to completely cover it. Trim off most of the excess napkin. Remove the napkin from the ball.

2 Mix one part water to three parts glue in the margarine tub. Roll the ball in the tub to completely cover it with the watery glue.

3 Carefully wrap the trimmed napkin around the wet ball to cover it.

4 Cut a 3-inch (7-cm) piece of pipe cleaner. Push the two ends into the top of the ball to make a hanger for the ornament.

5 Hold the ornament by the hanger and use the paintbrush to cover the outside of the ball with the watery glue. Sprinkle the entire ball with clear glitter. Let it dry completely in a Styrofoam egg carton. (This will allow it to dry with most of the surface of the ornament exposed to the air.)

Original ornaments are only as limited as your supply of different holiday napkins!

Feed the Birds Ornament

This ornament would make a great gift for someone who is especially fond of birds.

What you need:

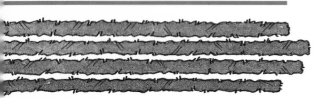

four 12-inch (30-cm) brown pipe cleaners

large flat button

masking tape

stickers or pictures of winter birds from old greeting cards

birdseed

fiberfill

white glue

scissors

gold thread

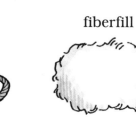

What you do:

1 Hold three of the pipe cleaners together and bend them in half. Twist the folded pipe cleaners together at the folded end to form a tree trunk. Spread the six ends of the pipe cleaners out to form the branches of the trees.

2 Cut the last pipe cleaner into pieces 1 to 3 inches (2 to 7 cm) long. Wrap the pieces around the branches of the tree to form smaller branches.

3 Slide the button onto one of the tree branches to make a tiny bird feeder. Put a little piece of masking tape on top of the button to make a better gluing surface. Cover the tape with glue and sprinkle it with birdseed.

4 Glue bits of fiberfill to the base of the tree and on the branches to look like snow.

5 Glue two or more small bird pictures or stickers on the branches of the tree.

6 Cut a 6-inch (15-cm) piece of gold thread. Tie the thread to the top of a center branch of the tree, then tie the two ends together to make a hanger for the ornament.

You might want to glue a little squirrel on your tree, too.

Dog Biscuit Doggie

If you make this doggie ornament for your favorite pooch, you'd better hang it up high or it might disappear!

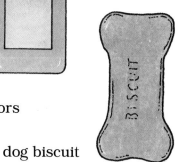

What you need:

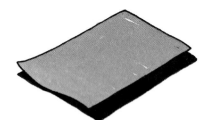

green and black felt scraps

two wiggle eyes

thin red ribbon

blue glue gel

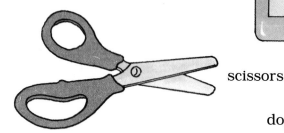

scissors

dog biscuit

brown pom-pom

red sequin

What you do:

 Cut a pair of floppy ears from the black felt. Glue the ears hanging down from one end of the front of the dog biscuit.

 Glue on two wiggle eyes below the ears.

 Glue the pom-pom nose to the other end of the biscuit.

 Cut two holly leaves from the green felt. Glue the leaves between the ears of the dog. Glue a sequin berry in the center of the leaves.

 Cut a 6-inch (15-cm) piece of ribbon. Glue the two ends of the ribbon to the back of the biscuit to make a hanger.

Woof, woof! That's dog talk for "Merry Christmas!"

Reindeer Treat Holder

Use an old party hat to make a container for candy and other small surprises.

What you need:

red or green poster paint and a paintbrush

old party hat

two large wiggle eyes

stapler

scissors

two 12-inch (30-cm) red pipe cleaners

glue

large red pom-pom

red felt scrap

red tissue paper

What you do:

1 If the party hat is not a solid color or is not the color you want, paint the outside of the hat red or green.

2 Turn the hat upside-down to form a container with an elastic handle.

3 Cut one of the red pipe cleaners in half. Staple one piece of the pipe cleaner to each side of the hat where the elastic is attached. These will be the antlers. Cut two 5-inch (13-cm) pieces from the second pipe cleaner. Wrap a piece around each antler to form the branches of the antlers.

4 Cut two ears from the red felt scrap. Glue them below the antlers.

5 Glue the two wiggle eyes about one third of the way down the hat.

6 Glue the red pom-pom nose on the front of the point of the hat.

Tuck a square of tissue inside the hat to hold some candies or other treats. One of these ornaments would make a nice gift for a friend.

Shank Button Wreath

Shank buttons, the ones with a small loop on the back, make beautiful wreath ornaments.

ꞋWhat you need:

nine shank buttons

12-inch (30-cm) green pipe cleaner

scissors

thin green ribbon

ꞋWhat you do:

1 Thread all of the buttons onto the pipe cleaner so that they are touching each other.

2 Center the buttons on the pipe cleaner and wrap the ends around each other to form a circle shape that is completely covered with buttons.

3 Use the excess pipe cleaner to form a small circle hanger at the top of the wreath. Trim off any extra pipe cleaner that you do not need.

4 Tie the green ribbon in a bow around the base of the hanger.

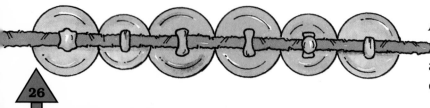

A collection of all different metal shank buttons makes an especially beautiful wreath ornament.

Bead and Bell Ornament

Many different looks can be achieved with this ornament by using beads of different colors and shapes.

What you need:

12-inch (30-cm) pipe cleaner

large jingle bell

small beads

What you do:

1 Fold the pipe cleaner in half. String the bell onto the pipe cleaner so that it hangs down from the fold.

2 String one bead over both pipe cleaners and slide it down to the bell. Next string

a bead on each pipe cleaner stem and slide them down until they are next to each other. Use any combination of these two methods to string the beads on the pipe cleaner.

3 Leave a 1½-inch (4-cm) piece of pipe cleaner on each side of the top of the ornament. Twist the two ends together to make a hanger for the ornament.

You might want to try stringing buttons or pasta instead of beads.

Handprint Reindeer

The little reindeer will remind you of just what size your hand was the Christmas you made it.

What you need:

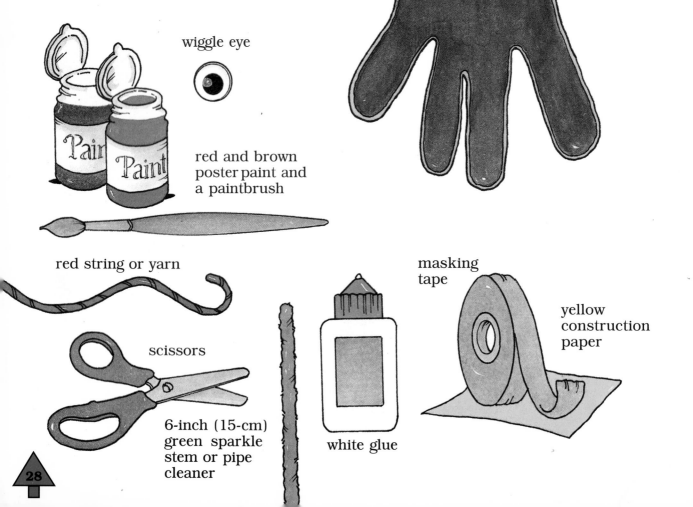

wiggle eye

red and brown poster paint and a paintbrush

red string or yarn

scissors

6-inch (15-cm) green sparkle stem or pipe cleaner

white glue

masking tape

yellow construction paper

What you do:

1 Hold your hand palm-up. Paint the tip of your thumb red. Paint the rest of your thumb, hand, and fingers brown.

2 Spread your thumb and fingers apart and make a handprint on the yellow paper.

3 When the paint has dried, cut out the handprint.

4 Your thumb is the head of the reindeer with a red nose. Glue a wiggle eye on the brown part of the thumb.

5 Cut a 4½-inch (1½-cm) piece from the pipe cleaner and fold it in half to make two antlers. Cut the remaining pipe cleaner in half. Wrap a piece around each antler to make the branches of the antler.

6 Glue the fold of the pipe cleaner behind the head of the reindeer so that the antlers stick out above the head. Use the masking tape to hold them in place while the glue dries.

7 Cut a 6-inch (15-cm) piece of red string. Tie the two ends together to make a loop. Glue the knot of the loop behind the reindeer to make a hanger for the ornament.

Write your name and the date on the back of the reindeer and give it to a special grown-up.

Tray of Cookies Ornament

Everyone likes Christmas cookies!

What you need:

corrugated
box cardboard

masking
tape

aluminum foil

white glue

scissors

red felt

shape punches such as
star, teddy bear, and
Christmas tree

thin red
ribbon

one or more
different
color glues

brown construction
paper scraps

What you do:

 1 Cut a rectangle from the cardboard about 2½ inches (6 cm) by 3½ inches (9 cm). Cover the cardboard with aluminum foil to make it look like a cookie sheet.

 2 Cut a 6-inch (15-cm) piece of ribbon. Tape the two ends to the back of one corner of the cookie sheet to make a hanger.

 3 Cover the back of the cookie sheet with masking tape to create a better gluing surface.

 4 Cut a 2½-inch (6-cm) by 3½-inch (9-cm) rectangle of felt and glue it to the back of the cookie sheet.

 5 Use the shape punches to cut little cookies from the brown paper.

 6 Put a tiny piece of masking tape over each place on the cookie sheet you want to put a cookie. Glue a cookie on each piece of tape.

 7 Use the colored glues to "frost" the cookies.

This little ornament looks so yummy that you'll want to make some real Christmas cookies to eat.

Peaceful Dove

*Fly this beautiful bird among
the branches of your tree.*

What you need:

three round
coffee filters

sharp black marker

thin red
ribbon

white glue

scissors

clamp clothespin

Styrofoam tray
for drying

6-inch (15-cm) green
pipe cleaner

What you do:

 Fold one coffee filter into quarters for the tail of the dove. Glue the tail to one side of the back handle half of the clothespin, with the pleated end sticking out past the clothespin.

 Fold the next filter into eighths for the head of the dove. Use the marker to draw an eye on each side of the head, and a beak. Glue the head to the front part of the same side of the clothespin as the tail, with the point sticking out beyond the front of the clothespin.

 Fold the last filter in half with glue between the folds to hold it in place. This will be the wings. Glue the wings over the top of the clothespin so that the end of the tail sticks out from the pleated end of the wings and the pointed head sticks out from the flat side of the wings.

 Shape a wreath 1½ inches (4 cm) wide from the green pipe cleaner by wrapping the pipe cleaner around and around itself in a circle.

 Tie a tiny bow from the red ribbon. Glue the bow to the wreath.

 Slip the beak of the dove between the layers of the wreath. Hold the wreath in place with a drop of glue.

Attach the dove to your tree by clamping it to a branch with the clothespin underneath it.

Foil Ring Ornament

This decoration is so easy you might want to try making it with a younger brother or sister.

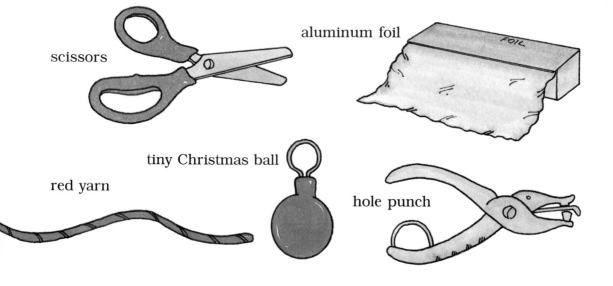

What you need:

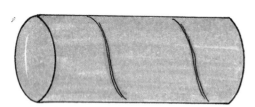

cardboard toilet-tissue tube

scissors

aluminum foil

red yarn

tiny Christmas ball

hole punch

What you do:

 1 Cut a 1-inch (2½-cm) band from the end of the cardboard tube.

 2 Cover the band both inside and out with aluminum foil.

 3 Punch a hole in the band.

 4 Cut an 8-inch (20-cm) piece of red yarn. String the colored ball onto the yarn.

 5 String the ends of the yarn through the hole from the inside of the tube to the outside so that the ball hangs down inside the band. Tie the two ends of the yarn together to make a hanger.

This ornament looks so pretty reflecting the lights on the tree. Try making some using jingle bells instead of the Christmas balls.

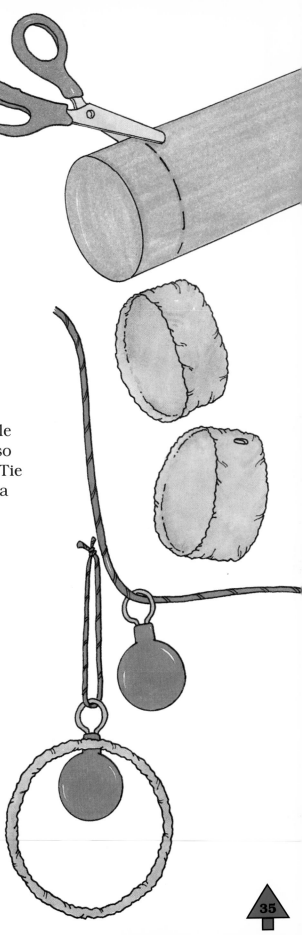

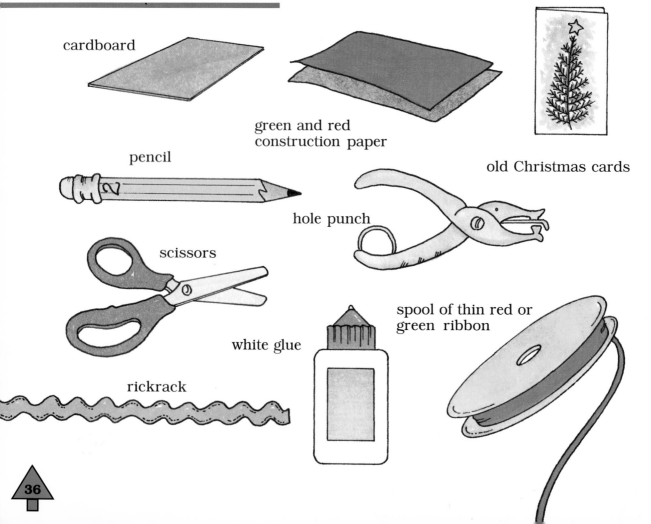

Circle Garland

Make this garland to drape around your tree.

What you need:

cardboard

green and red
construction paper

old Christmas cards

pencil

hole punch

scissors

spool of thin red or
green ribbon

white glue

rickrack

What you do:

1 Make a 2-inch (5-cm) circle pattern from the cardboard.

2 Use the pattern to cut out lots of circles from the construction paper. Punch two holes, about 1 inch (2½ cm) apart near the edge of each circle. This will be the top of the circle. Decorate each circle with rickrack.

3 Use the pattern to cut out picture circles from old Christmas cards. Make as many picture circles as you made construction paper circles. Punch two holes in the top of each circle.

4 Cut a piece of ribbon long enough to string all your circles on. Alternate picture circles and construction paper circles on the ribbon, threading the ribbon through the back of each hole, then down through the front of the second hole.

5 Tie off each end of the garland and wrap it around the branches of your tree.

Spaghetti Wreath

Did you ever think that spaghetti could turn into a pine wreath?

What you need:

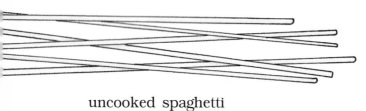

uncooked spaghetti

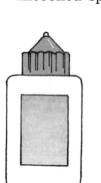

white glue

red nail polish

green food coloring

margarine tub with lid

hairpin

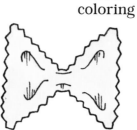

one piece of bow-tie pasta

craft stick

What you do:

1 Break spaghetti into ¼- to ½-inch (½- to 1-cm) pieces to get about ½ cup of spaghetti bits.

2 Use the craft stick to mix about ½ cup of glue with a few drops of green food coloring in the margarine tub.

3 Add the spaghetti bits to the glue and mix until the spaghetti is completely coated with green glue.

4 Shape the gluey spaghetti on the plastic lid in the shape of a 2½-inch (1½-cm) wreath. This ornament is best kept small because the pasta is quite heavy.

5 Slip a hairpin into one edge of the wreath to make a hanger.

6 Paint the bow-tie pasta red with the nail polish. Glue the red bow on the wreath.

When the wreath is completely dry, peel it off the plastic lid. It will take at least a day and maybe longer to dry.

Gingerbread Cookie Ornament

This cookie ornament smells good enough to eat!

What you need:

corrugated box cardboard

sequins

scissors

white glue

gingerbread person cookie cutter

cinnamon

tiny red pom-pom

pencil

thin red ribbon

red rickrack

Styrofoam tray to work on

What you do:

1 Trace around the cookie cutter on the cardboard. Cut out the gingerbread person shape.

2 Cover the shape with glue, then sprinkle it with cinnamon. Let the glue dry completely, then shake off any excess cinnamon.

3 Use the sequins to give the cookie person eyes and buttons. Glue on the pom-pom for a nose. Cut a tiny smile from the rickrack and glue it in place. Use strips of rickrack to decorate the head, arms, and legs.

4 Cut a 5-inch (13-cm) strip of ribbon. Glue the two ends of the ribbon to the back of the head of the gingerbread person to make a hanger for the ornament.

Do you smell freshly-baked cookies?

41

Christmas Bell

This little bell ornament really rings.

What you need:

paper napkin with Christmas pattern all over it

1½-inch (4-cm) Styrofoam ball

jingle bell

thin red ribbon

scissors

bowl and spoon for mixing

newspaper to work on

white glue

Styrofoam tray for drying

bathroom-size paper cup

red pipe cleaner

What you do:

1 Ask a grown-up to cut the Styrofoam ball in half for you.

2 Cut a 6-inch (15-cm) piece of ribbon. Thread the jingle bell onto the ribbon. Poke a hole in the bottom of the cup. Holding the cup upside down, thread the two ends of the ribbon up through the inside of the cup and through the hole so that the bell hangs down slightly below the rim of the cup.

3 Rub glue over the outer bottom of the cup and the ends of the ribbon. Stick the flat side of the Styrofoam ball over the bottom of the cup and the ribbon ends.

4 Mix about ½ cup of glue with a few drops of water. Open the napkin and gently swish it around in the glue to completely cover it. If you have a large napkin, you may want to cut it down first. You will need enough to cover the outside of the bell.

5 Drape the gluey napkin over the cup bell, shaping it to the cup. Trim off the extra napkin at the bottom.

6 Cut a 3-inch (8-cm) piece of pipe cleaner. Push the two ends of the pipe cleaner into the Styrofoam top of the bell to make a hanger.

Jingle bells, jingle bells...

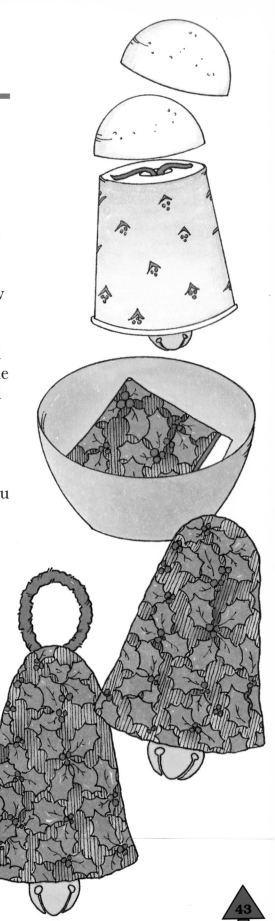

Wooden Spoon Snowman

Make this cold-weather friend from an old ice-cream spoon.

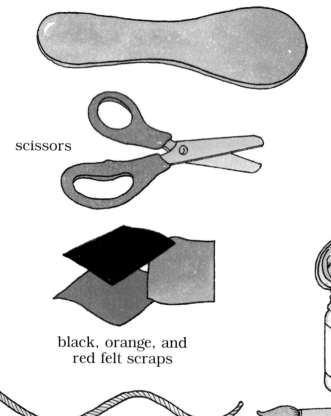

What you need:

wooden ice-cream spoon

scissors

white glue

black, orange, and red felt scraps

Styrofoam tray for drying

string

white poster paint with paintbrush

What you do:

1 Paint the ice-cream spoon white and let it dry.

2 The smaller, handle end of the spoon will be the head of the snowman. Cut out a hat, eyes, and buttons from the black felt and glue them in place. Cut a carrot nose from the orange felt and a scarf from the red felt and glue them on the snowman.

3 Cut a 5-inch (13-cm) piece of string. Glue the two ends between the snowman's hat and the spoon to make a hanger for the ornament.

This little fellow won't melt at the end of the season.

If you add a safety pin to his hat instead of the hanger, you can wear him as a pin.

Hands and Foot Angel

Turn your hands and foot shapes into a little angel.

What you need:

white and yellow construction paper

sequins or glitter

scissors

yellow pipe cleaner

yarn bits for hair

yarn

pencil

markers

white glue

construction paper in skin color of your choice

What you do:

 Trace around your bare foot on the white paper. Cut out the foot shape for the body of the angel.

 Trace around your hands on the yellow paper. Cut out the hand shapes for the wings of the angel. Glue the wings sticking out from each side of the middle portion of the foot.

 Cut a 2-inch (5-cm) circle from the skin-color construction paper for the head of the angel. Glue the head to the heel end of the foot shape on the opposite side that the wings are glued on.

 Shape a halo from the yellow pipe cleaner. Trim the end of the halo to about 2 inches (5 cm) long. Dip the end in glue and slip it between the top of the head and the body of the angel.

 Cut a 5-inch (13-cm) piece of yarn. Tie the yarn around the halo, then tie the two ends together to make a hanger for the angel.

 Use the markers to draw a face on the head of the angel. Cut yarn bits and glue them around the face for hair.

Decorate the halo, body, and wings of the angel with glitter and sequins.

Give the little angel to someone to remind them of another little angel . . . you, of course!

Tube Reindeer

This reindeer is so easy that you can make enough to pull Santa's sleigh in no time at all.

What you need:

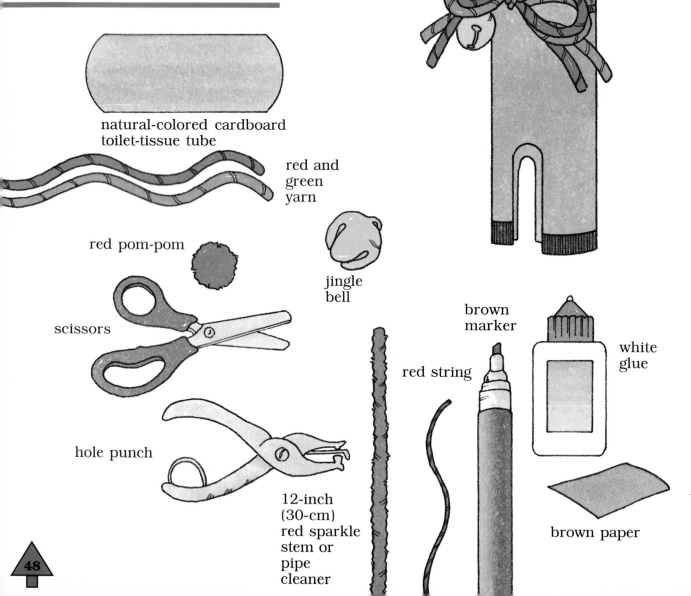

natural-colored cardboard toilet-tissue tube

red and green yarn

red pom-pom

jingle bell

scissors

hole punch

12-inch (30-cm) red sparkle stem or pipe cleaner

red string

brown marker

white glue

brown paper

What you do:

1 Cut four rectangles from the bottom edge of the tube that are 1½ inches (4 cm) high and ¼ inch (0.6 cm) wide and spaced equal distance apart around the edge of the tube. This will leave four pieces of tube hanging down for the reindeer legs. Color a brown hoof on the bottom of each leg.

2 Punch a hole in each side of the edge at the top of the tube. Cut the sparkle stem in half. Thread one half through the two holes, then bend each end up to form antlers. Cut the second piece of sparkle stem in half and wrap a piece around each antler to form the branches of the antlers.

3 Cut two ears for the reindeer from the brown paper. Glue them on the head below the antlers.

4 Draw two eyes with the brown marker. Glue on a red pom-pom for the nose.

5 Cut 8-inch (20-cm) pieces of red yarn and green yarn. Tie the two pieces of yarn around the neck of the reindeer and tie them in a knot. Thread the jingle bell onto one of the pieces of yarn and slide it down to the knot. Tie the yarn in a bow with the jingle bell hanging down from the bow.

6 Cut a 5-inch (13-cm) piece of string. Punch a hole in the back of the head of the reindeer. Thread the string through the hole and tie the two ends together to make a hanger for the ornament.

Hang the reindeer on the tree quickly, before it flies away!

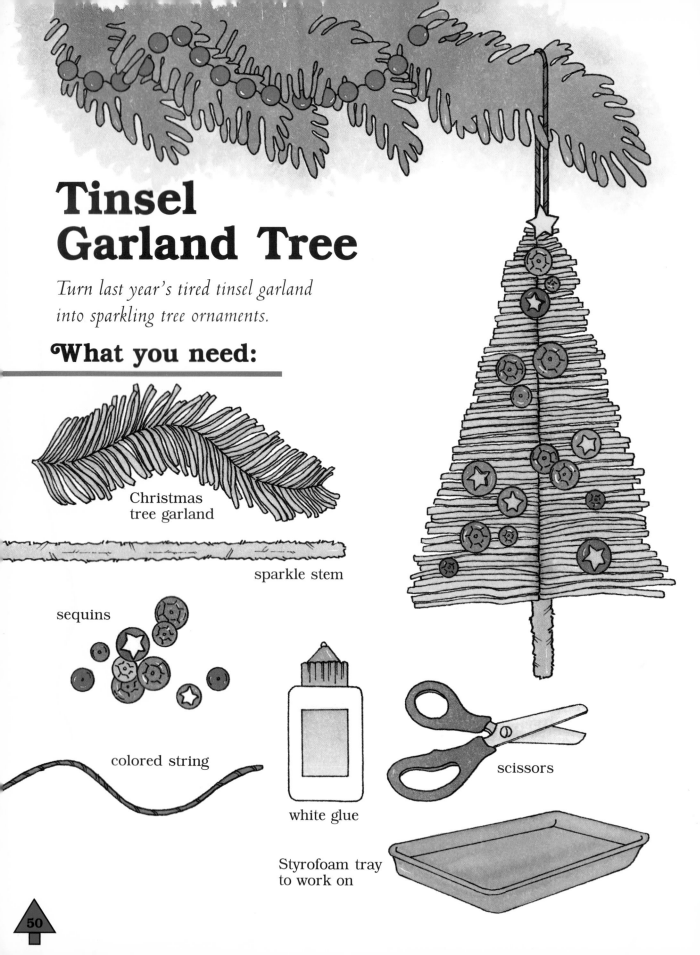

Tinsel Garland Tree

Turn last year's tired tinsel garland into sparkling tree ornaments.

What you need:

Christmas tree garland

sparkle stem

sequins

colored string

white glue

scissors

Styrofoam tray to work on

What you do:

1 Cut a 4-inch (10-cm) piece of sparkle stem for the trunk of the tree.

2 Cut a 6-inch (15-cm) piece of garland. Cut a 5-inch (13-cm) piece of string. Tie the string around the center of the piece of garland, then tie the two ends together to make a hanger.

3 Rub all of one side of the garland with glue. Fold the garland in half over one end of the sparkle stem to form the front and back of the tree with the hanger at the top.

4 Trim the two sides of the tree into a triangle to look like a Christmas tree.

5 Cover one side of the tree with glue and sprinkle with sequins to decorate. You might want to add a star-shaped sequin or sticker star at the top. Let the tree dry on the Styrofoam tray.

6 Turn the tree over and decorate the other side with sequins.

This tree makes a nice refrigerator magnet. Just decorate one side, leave off the hanger, and add one piece of sticky-backed magnet to the back.

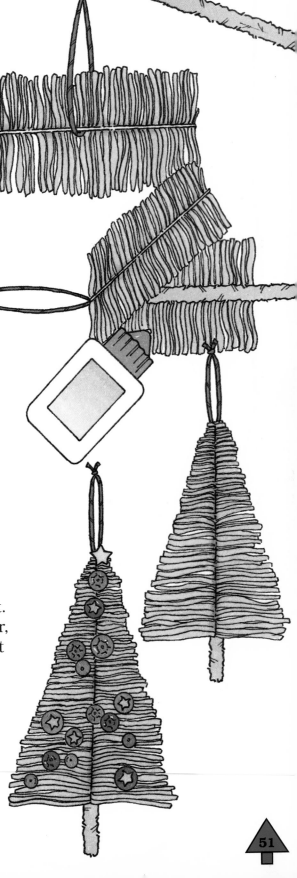

Christmas Stocking

Use the fingers from an old knit glove to make miniature Christmas stockings.

What you need:

old knit glove

two tiny wiggle eyes

fiberfill

rickrack

white glue

scissors

red and white pipe cleaners

small pom-pom

three tiny pom-poms

What you do:

1 Cut a finger from the glove to use as the stocking. Stuff the finger with fiberfill, pushing the stuffing in the fingertip over to one side to resemble the foot of a stocking.

2 Cut a 2-inch (5-cm) piece from both the red and the white pipe cleaners. Twist the two different colors together to make a little candy cane. Dip the end of the candy cane in glue and slide it down in one side of the stocking, between the fiberfill and the stocking.

3 Make a tiny teddy bear to peek out of the other side of the stocking. For its head, glue the small pom-pom on top of the fiberfill next to the candy cane. Glue on two tiny pom-pom ears, two tiny eyes, and a pom-pom nose.

4 Glue fiberfill around the top rim of the stocking. Decorate around the fiberfill with rickrack.

5 Cut a 3-inch (8-cm) piece of pipe cleaner. Tuck the two ends down into the stocking behind the teddy bear to make a hanger for the ornament.

This little stocking looks like a Christmas surprise for a mouse!

Berry Basket Snowflakes

Make a snowman's favorite ornament.

What you need:

plastic
berry basket

clear glitter

plastic bowl
for mixing

Styrofoam tray
to work on

white glue

water

paintbrush

facial
tissue

scissors

green yarn

What you do:

1 Cut the sides out of the basket. Cut three branched stems from the side and bottom of the basket.

2 Mix about ¼ cup of white glue with a small amount of water to thin it enough to paint the delicate tissue.

3 Spread the tissue out on the Styrofoam tray. Paint the tissue carefully with the watery glue. Arrange the three berry basket stems on top of the tissue, crisscrossing them to make a snowflake.

4 Cover the snowflake with another tissue. Dab the top tissue with more glue to completely cover the snowflake and the area around the snowflake.

5 Sprinkle the snowflake with the clear glitter. Let the project dry overnight.

6 When the tissue has dried completely, peel it off the tray. Trim away the excess tissue around the outside of the snowflake.

7 Cut a 5-inch (13-cm) piece of yarn. Tie the two ends together to make a hanger. Glue the hanger along the back of the snowflake with the loop sticking up from the top.

It is important to glue the hanger straight along the stem of one of the snowflake arms so that the ornament will hang straight.

Necktie Reindeer

This reindeer can be used as an ornament or a lapel pin. Maybe you should make more than one!

What you need:

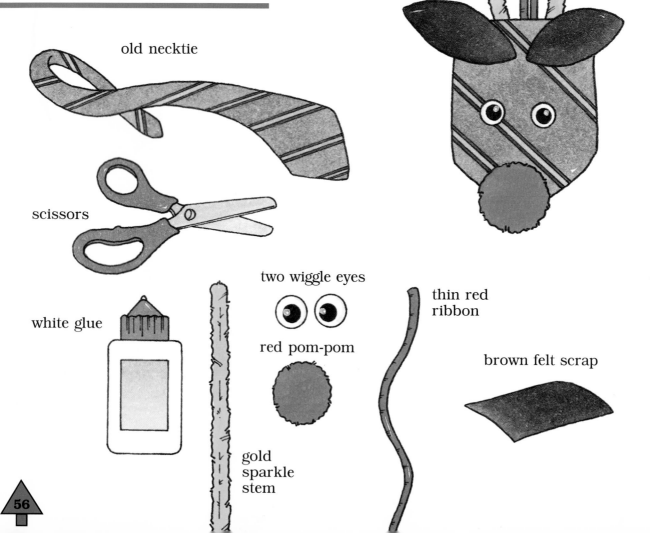

old necktie

scissors

white glue

two wiggle eyes

red pom-pom

gold sparkle stem

thin red ribbon

brown felt scrap

What you do:

 Cut a piece off the small end of the necktie about 1½ inches (4 cm) long, not including the point. This will be the head of the reindeer.

 Cut a 6-inch (15-cm) piece of sparkle stem and fold it in half for the antlers. Cut the remaining piece in half. Wrap one piece around the upper part of each antler to form the branches of the antlers. Glue the fold of the antlers between the front and back of the tie sticking up from the straight cut end.

 Cut two ears from the brown felt. Glue them to the head just below the antlers.

 Glue the two wiggle eyes on the head below the ears.

 Glue the red pom-pom on the point of the necktie for the nose.

6 Cut a 4-inch (10-cm) piece of red ribbon. Glue the two ends of the ribbon at the top of the reindeer head between the front and back of the tie.

If you want to use your reindeer as a pin, just add a safety-pin to the back instead of a ribbon hanger.

Poinsettia Ornament

The poinsettia is a traditional plant of the Christmas season.

What you need:

cardboard egg carton

gold sequins

scissors

Styrofoam tray to work on

gold thread

red and green poster paint and a paintbrush

white glue

What you do:

1 Cut two cups from the egg carton. Cut five points around the edge of one of the cups for the red top of the plant. Cut four points around the edge of the second cup for the green leaves underneath.

2 Paint the five-point cup red. Paint the four-point cup green. Gently open the damp points partway and let them dry.

3 Cut a 5-inch (13-cm) piece of gold thread. Glue the red cup over the green cup with the ends of the thread in between them to make a hanger for the ornament.

4 Make a center for the flower by gluing several gold sequins in the middle of the red cup.

You can make just one poinsettia to hang or make three of them to glue together in a cluster for a larger ornament.

Photo Locket Ornament

Hang a picture of you on the Christmas tree!

What you need:

two identical small lids, such as from baby-food jars

BABY FOOD

red nail polish

nail polish

white glue

scissors

a small photo of you

green ribbon

red and green rickrack

plastic lid for drying

green sticker stars

masking tape

green construction paper scrap and red felt scrap

What you do:

1 Paint both lids outside and around the inner edges with the red nail polish. Let the lids dry on the plastic lid.

2 Cut a 3- by ½-inch (8- by 1½-cm) rectangle of felt for a hinge between the two lids. Cover the inside of each lid with masking tape to create a better gluing surface. Glue one end of the hinge inside each lid.

3 Trace around the lid on the construction paper. Cut out the circle and trim it to fit inside one lid. Center the circle over the image you want to show on your photo and trace around it. Cut out the photo.

4 Cover the ends of the hinges with masking tape. Glue the circle of construction paper in the top lid and a photo inside the bottom lid.

5 Decorate the outside of both lids with the rickrack and stars.

6 Cut a 5-inch (13-cm) piece of ribbon. Tie the ribbon around the felt hinge between the two lids, then tie the ends together to make a hanger for the ornament.

Photo lockets make a nice Christmas surprise for someone special in your life. You could use two photos and make a gift from you and your brother or sister.

Paper Filter Angel

Fly an angel among the branches of your tree.

What you need:

round, white coffee filter

¾-inch (2-cm) wooden craft bead

white glue

two wiggle eyes

scissors

two white craft feathers

gold sparkle stem

gold thread

yarn for hair

red thread

gold stars

What you do:

1 To make the dress, fold the filter down around itself and twist the center. Dip the twist in glue and stick it in the hole in the bead, which will be the head of the angel.

2 Cut a 3-inch (8-cm) piece of sparkle stem. Shape the stem into a halo and slip the end into the hole at the top of the head. Squeeze a drop of glue in the hole to secure the halo.

3 Cut a 4-inch (10-cm) piece of gold thread. Slide the two ends down in the gluey hole with the halo to make a hanger for the ornament.

4 Cut yarn bits and glue them on the head for hair. Glue on the two wiggle eyes. Cut a tiny piece of red thread and glue it on the face in the shape of a smile.

5 Glue the two feathers sticking out from the back of the angel for wings.

6 Decorate the angel's dress with gold stars.

You might want to add other decorations to the angel's dress such as sequins or glitter.

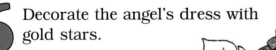

About the Author and Illustrator

Twenty years as a teacher and director of nursery school programs has given Kathy Ross extensive experience in guiding young children through crafts projects. Among the many craft books she has written are *Gifts to Make for Your Favorite Grownup, Crafts From Your Favorite Fairy Tales,* and *The Best Holiday Crafts Ever!*

Sharon Lane Holm, a resident of New Fairfield, Connecticut, won awards for her work in advertising design before shifting her concentration to children's books. Among the books she has illustrated recently are *Sidewalk Games Around the World* and *Happy Birthday, Everywhere,* both by Arlene Erlbach, and *Beautiful Bats* by Linda Glaser.

Together, Kathy Ross and Sharon Lane Holm have also created the popular Holiday Crafts for Kids series, as well as the Crafts for Kids Who Are Wild About series, both published by The Millbrook Press.